Musings of a Butterfly

Clarissa Evans

BookLeaf
Publishing

Presentation by *BookLeaf Publishing*

Web: www.bookleafpub.com

E-mail: info@bookleafpub.com

ISBN: 9789357617383

First edition 2022

For my baby girl. . .

Don't ever lose sight of your dreams

Who I Am

I am . . .
     the last grandchild
     the one who grew up without
grandparents
     always listening to other's memories
     the one without the joy

I am . . .
     the hardest child
     so hard to control
   never there, but always on time
     determined to live my best life

I am . . .
     the baby girl
     the sun that forgot to shine
     on the wrong life journey
     marching to my own drummer

I am . . .
   Mama, Mommy, Mom
   her only parent
   the one who keeps her safe
   that little girl's superhero

A Dream Delayed

Fighting for a comeback
One letter
One word
Taking it all back
One line
One stanza
This dream is mine!

Today

3

Today, I quit complaining!
Today, I quit being overwhelmed!
Today, I quit blaming others!
Today, I quit finding excuses!
Today, I quit waiting for the next best!
Today, I quit being envious of others!

Today, I take back my life!
Today, I take back my future!
Today, I take back my optimism!
Today, I take back my sanity!
Today, I take back my happy!

Today, I take ME back!

Butterfly Daydreams

Climbing, crawling
along the ground
Couldn't look up
I was so down

Confined, dark,
restricted and alone
Comforting, familiar
fear of the unknown

Isolated, healing,
coming into the light
Built anew
butterfly take flight

Haiku #3

5

Fluttering about
Gentle, delicate, quiet
Playful butterfly

To A Younger Me

Beautiful butterfly
Don't let your fears take over
This is just a season

You cannot let this encapsulate you
In time it will be as though
None of this ever happened

You must have extreme patience
And with lots of prayer
God is going to bless you

His most precious gift
Will be placed in your arms
Finally, you will be complete

Homeless

Everyday I walk between these cars
Wind, rain, hurricane
I carry this sign
All I want is what's mine.

Together Now Apart

It was no secret
You were up to no good
Promised me a future
Little girls dream about

That was our story
But I knew it had to end
You had so many ways to use me
And many more ways to hurt

You couldn't be trusted
I had to draw the line
Your tales of marriage and family
Put me out of my mind

I finally let you know
I knew your game
Knew it all along
Time to put an end to this

Now you're so far gone
Another statistic in the books
Killed by the cops
Can't believe you got shot

Have You Seen My Unicorn?

Looking for a unicorn
Such a magical creature
Thought I found one once
But it was just a horse

Looking for a unicorn
Going to find one soon
Spread magic all around
Live in the enchanted land

Looking for a unicorn
Need a mythical bait
One look and he'll know
Kindred spirits in a fairy tale

Haiku #1

Once it is over
Never a second thought
No one wants me back

First Love

Sometimes he stops by for a visit
So many memories we shared
The only bad day was our last

Whenever he's near my heart
I'm warm and cozy inside
Reminiscing on his tender embrace

There's never been another like him
A love that can never be replaced
Always together in my dreams

Neighbors

A perfect match
The neighbor from across the way
Three long years
They barely said hey

A few weeks before the big move
Text messages and phone calls
Finally getting acquainted
A spark of hope this could be more

A promise to call
Not a sound to be heard
Couldn't just tell the truth
They weren't friends anymore

Super Mommy

Her Mommy created this whole world
She thinks I'm good at everything
Call me the perfect Mommy
She doesn't know this is a disguise

Every morning upon her awakening
My invisible cape of Super Mommy appears
Suddenly all my fears fade away
All the imperfections no longer exist

But when she starts to cry
The cracks begin to show
What's wrong with my baby
The forcefield isn't working

I run to her, hug her tight
Mommy's here now, baby
Wanting to cry with her
Show her that Mommy is real

Like Sisters

The love of two cousins
Wanting so badly to be

Secrets kept from one
Forcing hidden truths from the other

A strange magnetism draws them in
Not knowing the bond

They will always be united
They have always been

A mother they have in common
Sisters by blood

A Mother's Love

One child
Two mothers
One mother by birth
The other a mother by love

Mommy by birth
Way too young to raise a child
No idea where to start
A decision she didn't want to make

Mommy by love
Prayed for a child
Didn't think it would ever happen
Now she has the greatest blessing

Both mothers grateful
A baby girl with so much love
A second chance
For all three

Haiku #2

Smiling, giggling
Not a care in the world
Baby innocence

Releasing Myself

I have plenty of stories to share
They walk around with me
Tapping me on the shoulder
Saying "remember when. . ."

Yes, I remember
Writing is what I forgot
An embellished tale here and there
Humiliation for practicing my craft

Now everyday speeds by
Afraid of what may come out
If I have a few minutes
To release these aching thoughts

Yes, I remember
Writing was the ultimate release
So many stories buried inside
Now they all come alive

Love Poetry

My roots are in poems
Dickenson showed me the way
Frost guided me along the path
But I still got lost

Stuck on writing a story
But there's no story within
Poetry is my passion
It's where I begin